Late-Blooming Cherries

Praise for *Late-Blooming Cherries*

'The standard of writing is exceptional ... Observations of ordinary life and relationships between humanity and nature are elevated to a level that feels extraordinary, magical ... These haiku feed our hearts and our minds.'

—Lynne Rees, co-editor, *Another Country: Haiku Poetry from Wales*

'Delightfully titled ... masterful, bold, all-encompassing ... and well-edited.'

—David McMurray, Professor of Haiku Studies, International University of Kagoshima, Japan

'A flowering for the English-language haiku community of India.'

—John Stevenson, managing editor, *The Heron's Nest*, Nassau, USA

'Very much of its home country ... as complex and varied as the country's diverse population. A necessary volume.'

—Paul Miller, editor, *Modern Haiku*, Lincoln, USA

Late-Blooming Cherries

~HAIKU POETRY FROM INDIA~

Edited by

KYNPHAM SING NONGKYNRIH
AND RIMI NATH

HarperCollins *Publishers* India

First published in India by HarperCollins *Publishers* 2024
4th Floor, Tower A, Building No. 10, DLF Cyber City,
DLF Phase II, Gurugram, Haryana – 122002
www.harpercollins.co.in

2 4 6 8 10 9 7 5 3 1

Anthology Copyright © Kynpham Sing Nongkynrih and
Rimi Nath 2024

Copyright for the individual pieces vests with the respective
contributors

P-ISBN: 978-93-5699-996-1
E-ISBN: 978-93-5699-729-5

This is a work of fiction and all characters and incidents described
in this book are the product of the author's imagination. Any
resemblance to actual persons, living or dead, is entirely coincidental.

The individual contributors assert the moral right
to be identified as the authors of their works.

All rights reserved. No part of this publication may be reproduced,
stored in a retrieval system, or transmitted, in any form or by any
means, electronic, mechanical, photocopying, recording or otherwise,
without the prior permission of the publishers.

Typeset in 11/16 Aldine401 BT at
Manipal Technologies Limited, Manipal

Printed and bound at
Thomson Press (India) Ltd

This book is produced from independently certified FSC® paper
to ensure responsible forest management.

under the cherry tree—
blossom soup,
blossom salad.
Bashō

Contents

Foreword ix
Introduction xi
A Note on the Haiku xviii

Late-Blooming Cherries: Poets

Muskaan Ahuja 3
Priti Aisola 7
G. Akila 9
Sanjuktaa Asopa 11
R. Suresh Babu 16
Ram Chandran 18
Mallika Chari 21
Geetashree Chatterjee 25
Kanchan Chatterjee 27
Salil Chaturvedi 31
Anannya Dasgupta 34

Shashi Angelee Deodhar	36
Kanjini Devi	40
Baisali Chatterjee Dutt	42
Kinshuk Gupta	44
Lakshmi Iyer	47
Rohini Gupta	49
Surashree Joshi	55
Abhay K.	57
Sushama Kapur	62
Arvinder Kaur	64
Suhit Kelkar	70
Ravi Kiran	72
Anju Kishore	74
Neha R. Krishna	76
Shobhana Kumar	79
Johannes Manjrekar	83
Daipayan Nair	88
Priya Narayanan	91
Indra Neil	93
Subir Ningthouja	96
Rimi Nath	98

Kynpham Sing Nongkynrih	104
Pravat Kumar Padhy	111
Aparna Pathak	114
Vandana Parashar	116
Shalini Pattabiraman	119
Madhuri Pillai	121
Amrutha Prabhu	124
Raamesh Gowri Raghavan	126
Brijesh Raj	128
Geethanjali Rajan	131
Milan Rajkumar	137
K. Ramesh	140
Kala Ramesh	146
Srinivas S.	152
Srinivas Rao Sambangi	155
Minal Sarosh	158
Joe Sebastian	162
Teji Sethi	166
Shloka Shankar	172
Kashiana Singh	175
Neena Singh	178

Ram Krishna Singh	182
A. Thiagarajan	186
Paresh Tiwari	190
Anitha Varma	195
Vidya S. Venkatramani	200

Foreword

These haiku and senryu by writers from India transcend all geographical, social and cultural boundaries and enter the experience of the readers, no matter where they might live. They echo and shiver with moments observed, imagined and remembered. They explore the pragmatic and the metaphysical with humour, heartbreak, profound insight and a serious appreciation of language, chosen for its precision and suggestiveness.

Observations of ordinary life and relationships between humanity and nature are elevated to a level that feels extraordinary, magical. The beauty is, at times, visceral. The haiku remind me that wherever I am in my life, wherever I am in the world, I can never be alone because I am always connected to something, someone.

'*blossom soup / blossom salad*' are the words from Bashō's haiku at the beginning of the anthology. Soup nurtures. Salad refreshes. And that's exactly how I felt after reading *Late-Blooming Cherries*. These haiku feed our hearts and our minds.

Lynne Rees
(Co-editor, *Another Country: Haiku Poetry from Wales*)

Introduction

late-blooming cherries
by the highway—how else
can I describe my haiku?

The title of *Late-Blooming Cherries: Haiku Poetry from India* was inspired by the haiku quoted above, from *Time's Barter: Haiku and Senryu*. The poem is related to the poet's late-blooming haiku and to a species of cherry tree popularly known as late bloomer, which blossoms in Shillong in early December. These cherry trees were brought from Japan to Shillong by the Meghalaya Forests and Environment Department in the 1970s. But while the cherry trees of Japan generally blossom in spring, here, because of the warmer climate, the cherries usually 'turned the town pink with their blush' ('A Farewell Letter of Cherries') in late autumn. The late bloomers, however, do not flower with the rest. They begin blooming only towards early winter. On the topic of late bloomers, David McMurray, Professor of Haiku Studies at the International University of Kagoshima, Japan, says:

> After the petals from common varieties of cherry trees have fallen, late-blooming cherry trees named *yae zakura* in Japan mature. Their blossoms arrive later and stay longer. A warming climate is forcing the petals of the demure *somei yoshino* to open up one month earlier than usual in Kyoto, so later-blooming varieties have become much more popular in Japan. In face of the hardships of climate change, these late-bloomers have developed resilience and sustainability.

Our *Late-Blooming Cherries* is so named because it is long overdue in its coming. The idea for it struck us after we reread *Another Country: Haiku Poetry from Wales* (2011), edited by Nigel Jenkins, Ken Jones and Lynne Rees. We realized with a sudden eagerness that should we bring out an anthology such as *Another Country*, it would be the first-ever haiku anthology in English from India. Our eagerness galvanized us into action and we embarked upon the long process of preparing the anthology almost immediately.

The first bilingual haiku anthology (Hindi–English) from India is, of course, Dr Shashi Angelee Deodhar's seventy-two-page *Indian Haiku: A Bilingual Anthology of Haiku*, published in 2008. But it is not an exclusively English-language haiku anthology. Kala Ramesh et al. also edited *Naad Anunaad: An Anthology of Contemporary World Haiku*, published in 2016. But this, as the name suggests, is not exclusively Indian. There have also been one or two other publications featuring haiku (like the *Katha* and *Hawakal* anthologies), but none exclusively.

Retracing the history of haiku in India, Deodhar, in her article 'Haiku: An Indian Perspective', published by *Simply Haiku* in autumn 2005, acknowledged the significant contributions of some of India's most revered poets and writers at the beginning of the twentieth century. According to her, Rabindranath Tagore and Subramania Bharati 'wrote eloquently about Japanese culture and literary heritage'. Tagore even wrote haiku-like poems, collected in his *Fireflies* and *Particles, Jottings, Sparks: The Collected Brief Poems*. India's 'first Japanese scholar', Prof. Satya Bhushan Verma, translated the first book of Japanese haiku (*Japani Kavitaian*) into Hindi in 1977 and, in 1981, started a newsletter in Hindi called *Haiku*.

Triveni Haikai, which represents the most important community of haiku lovers and practitioners in India, also acknowledges the contributions of Prof. B.S. Aggarwala and Dr Angelee Deodhar, who 'worked tirelessly to popularise haiku, though mainly in the Hindi-speaking belt of northern India'[1]. Prof. Aggarwala also started a Hindi quarterly called *Haiku Bharati* in 1998.

---

1 https://www.trivenihaikai.in/about-us

Haiku in India, whether in English or the vernacular languages, is yet to flourish in the same way as mainstream poetry. Although some Indian journals are publishing haiku poetry, and one or two national publishers have brought out an occasional book of haiku, the genre is yet to gain popularity among the major poets and writers of the country. As we have discovered, not many established poets have been featured in any of the prominent haiku journals. Even in this anthology, only eleven poets are equally adept at both haiku and mainstream poetry. Another important fact is that we have in this anthology only fifty-seven haiku poets, including five living overseas. Admittedly, the selection has been stringent and only what we consider the best has been included. Still, if this had been an anthology of Indian English poetry, the number of first-rate poets would have run into hundreds, if not thousands. This, therefore, makes *Late-Blooming Cherries* an even more important intervention.

One of the best things about this pioneering venture is that the editors' excitement is almost matched by the enthusiasm of the contributors, some of whom helped us with the contact details of many of the haikuists here. Among the enthusiastic helpers are Kala Ramesh, Geethanjali Rajan, Shloka Shankar, Madhuri Pillai and Milan Rajkumar. Nandini Manjrekar and Ananth Deodhar helped us with the haiku of the late Dr Angelee Deodhar and Johannes Manjrekar. We are sincerely thankful to them and to all those who contributed, in one way or another, to the 'flowering' of *Late-Blooming Cherries*. Among them are David McMurray, Lynne Rees, John Stevenson and Paul Miller. Meghan MacNeil gave us permission to use one of Paul MacNeil's poems. We are deeply grateful to her.

In our selection, we have tried to include as many of the best haiku poets as possible. The haiku in the anthology have been selected primarily because of their quality, though we admit that this could be highly subjective. The maximum number of haiku by a poet here is twenty; the minimum is five. We believe that this anthology is quite comprehensive, presenting a definitive account of the state of haiku writing in India. While haiku and senryu are Japanese forms, the themes of the poetry here are typically

Indian and universally human. We hope that the readers enjoy reading them as much as we did selecting them.

The only advice we would like to give our readers is to keep in mind that haiku poetry is like lappraw. Lappraw, as the narrator of the novel *Funeral Nights* says, 'is one of those showers that comes and ends abruptly. You have to be absolutely absorbed to enjoy [the experience]. It is over before you know it'[2]. This is exactly what the haiku experience is like. Therefore, to borrow the words of the editors of *Another Country*, 'Please chew slowly' if you want to 'release the full flavour'[3] of the feast in *Late-Blooming Cherries*.

Kynpham Sing Nongkynrih
Rimi Nath
Shillong, 13 July 2022

---

2 Kynpham Sing Nongkynrih. *Funeral Nights* (Westland/Context, 2021).
3 Lynne Rees. *Another Country: Haiku Poetry from Wales* (Gomer Press, 2011).

A Note on the Haiku

The oldest anthologies of Japanese poetry date back to the eighth century CE; however, it was not until the seventeenth century that the haiku emerged as one of the most beloved poetic forms.[1] In its literal translation from the Japanese language, it simply means 'light verse'. According to well-known British critic Chris Baldick, the haiku 'is a form of Japanese lyric verse that encapsulates a single impression of a natural object or scene, within a particular season', and is written in 'seventeen syllables arranged in three

---

1 David McMurray. *Haiku Composed in English as a Japanese Language* (International University of Kagoshima Press, 2003), pp. 4–5.

unrhymed lines of five, seven, and five syllables'.[2] The following is one of Bashō's haiku translated in the traditional format:

> *in the twilight rain*
> *these brilliant-hued hibiscus—*
> *a lovely sunset.*[3]

The haiku is derived from the word hokku, which means 'starting verse'. The hokku is an opening stanza of a longer poetic form called haikai-no-renga. During the seventeenth century and the one that followed, the hokku flourished in the hands of Matsuo Bashō (1644–94), Yosa Buson (1716–84) and Kobayashi Issa (1763–1828). These three masters wrote the kind of haiku described by Baldick above, which evoked feelings never directly stated, only suggested through natural images. In other words, their hokku revealed the world of nature as it was

---

[2] Chris Baldick. *The Concise Oxford Dictionary of Literary Terms* (New York: Oxford University Press, 1990), p. 95.

[3] Matsuo Bashō. 'In the twilight rain' (Poetry Soup.com).

before the mechanized age, as in this haiku by Bashō:

> *friends part*
> *forever—wild geese*
> *lost in cloud.*[4]

Near the end of the nineteenth century, the hokku was completely separated from the haikai and renamed haiku. Well-known Welsh writer and authority on haiku poetry Nigel Jenkins says that even now the haiku lives fully in nature because 'whatever its subject it never allows us to forget that we, no less than that spider or this droplet of water, are part of the living cosmos'[5]. But at the same time, the haiku shows us facets of a changing world. By focusing on the moment, it is naturally bound to reflect changes in our social and cultural life, and 'has moved effortlessly into the street, the factory, the office, the airport, and

---

4 Matsuo Bashō. *Haiku* (London: Penguin Books, 1985), p. 51.
5 Nigel Jenkins. 'Introduction', in Kynpham Sing Nongkynrih, *Time's Barter: Haiku and Senryu* (New Delhi: HarperCollins, 2015), pp. ix–xxiii.

may cast its wise, forgiving eye on almost any aspect of modern life'[6].

Another important change in the contemporary haiku can be seen in its form. According to Baldick, Japanese haiku were traditionally written in 'seventeen syllables arranged in three unrhymed lines of five, seven, and five syllables'. Haiku written in English and other non-Japanese languages also used a similar form. But this metre is no longer strictly observed. Jenkins believes that in languages such as English, whose grammar is heavily dependent on word order, haiku may work better by departing from its strict metrical form. Japanese as a language, he says, 'is grammatically far more malleable, and thus easier to fit into a rigid form such as 5-7-5'[7]. Even though that is the case, the Japanese themselves were the first to have experimented with the form more than a hundred years ago, by straying from the haiku's metrical provisions. As time passed, and as haiku began to be written in many other

---

6 Ibid.
7 Ibid.

languages around the world, it was recognized more and more that its fundamental quality is to express the poet's experience in the fewest words possible. This is also related to the fact that Japanese haikuists were largely influenced by Zen Buddhism, which teaches the principle of 'More is less.'[8] The strict 5-7-5 rule is thus hardly followed in contemporary English haiku anymore:

> *all the times*
> *I have been wrong*
> *fresh paint*[9]
> —Lynne Rees

There are also many poets today writing their haiku in the single-line or double-line form. Others have been known to use as many as four lines.

Brevity, economy, concision and simplicity are thus the most fundamental elements of good

---

8 David Crystal, ed. *The New Penguin Encyclopedia* (New Delhi: Penguin Books India, 2002), p. 1675.
9 Lynne Rees. *Another Country: Haiku Poetry from Wales* (Gomer Press, 2011), p. 16.

haiku. They articulate the poet's experience through words having a present-tense immediacy and the quality of high suggestiveness. This suggestive quality is chiefly owing to the presence of imagery, which the haiku cannot do without. The best haiku poets writing today try to capture these qualities without fretting too much about the traditional metre.

In his elucidation of the haiku, Bashō especially focused on the importance of the poet's intuitive experience. He said that the haiku 'is simply what is happening in this place, at this moment'[10] and how it affects the poet's feelings. The haiku does not preoccupy itself with questions of philosophy, religion, politics or ideology. It minutely examines things that happen at a particular place, at a particular moment, revealing the poet's feelings through images drawn from nature. The haiku moment, as Jenkins says, is brief and precise but never

---

10 From Bashō's comments on the haiku as quoted by Jenkins. See Nigel Jenkins. 'Introduction', *Time's Barter: Haiku and Senryu*, p. xxii.

obscure or perplexing; its language is always simple and colloquial.

In this way, the haiku encourages us to pay special attention to every little creature or little thing usually considered insignificant in our daily lives, such as a bulbul on a plum tree, a caterpillar on a wall, raindrops on an arum leaf, or the moon and the stars in the night sky. This is how we are made to respect and value all of God's creations, big and small, and 'to look not at it, but as it' as in the teachings of Zen Buddhism. It is for this reason that renowned Welsh writer Tony Conran observed that the essential qualities of the haiku are 'loneliness, tenderness and slenderness'[11].

With regard to its form, the haiku, as we understand it, is made up of two parts. One is the setting, which presents an image that is not only the background but also the foundation of the poem. According to Ferris Gilli, the backdrop

---

11 From Tony Conran's essay, 'Haiku as an English Poetic Form: A Personal Approach'. See Nigel Jenkins. 'Introduction', *Time's Barter: Haiku and Senryu*, p. xvi.

may be in the shape of 'a place' (as in, a garden or a courtyard), 'an occasion' (for example, a birthday, New Year or a new job), 'the weather', 'the time of day', 'an action or activity' (such as the chirping of birds or the blowing of the wind) and 'any other thing' (for instance, the sunrise or the sunset).[12]

The other part is the body, which contains not only the most important but the longest part of the haiku (although this may not always be so), forming the rock bottom or the heart of the poem. It is here that the subject and the action of the haiku are expressed. Consider the following example:

> *bird of time—*
> *in Kyoto*
> *pining for Kyoto.*
> —Bashō[13]

---

12 Ferris Gilli. 'Spring Dusk', *Frogpond* (Nassau XXVI: 2001).
13 Matsuo Bashō. *Haiku* (London: Penguin Books, 1985), p. 24.

The first line constitutes the setting, while the lines that follow are the body, containing the subject and the action. Sometimes the setting may spill over to the second line as in the following example:

> *from the heart*
> *of the sweet peony,*
> *a drunken bee.*
> —Bashō[14]

In these component parts, the haiku may contain two images, forming the setting and the body. These images are not only different from each other but may also be quite contradictory. It is this peculiar nature of the images that brings about the quality of juxtaposition and contrast in all haiku. When viewed casually, the images may appear to speak about subjects that seem to have nothing to do with each other. But they are, in fact, a commentary on one another, as in the following haiku by Paul MacNeil:

---

14 Ibid, p. 56.

jacaranda flowers—
the twin tracks
of a car.[15]

Here, the jacaranda flowers and the tracks of a car do not seem to be related. Flowers are objects of nature while the tyres are human artefacts. But when examined carefully, we discover that the image in the body of the haiku is actually a comment on the image in the setting, which illustrates how man destroys the things that nature creates.

We must also keep in mind that not all haiku contain images that carry the quality of juxtaposition and contrast. Many speak about their diverse subjects in diverse ways, as the following example from Bashō may illustrate:

early autumn:
rice field, ocean,
one green.[16]

---

15 Paul MacNeil. *The Heron's Nest* (Port Townsend II: 5, 2000).
16 Matsuo Bashō. *Haiku* (London: Penguin Books, 1985), p. 20.

Here, the image of the setting identifies the time and the season, while that of the body simply explains the things that occur in that time or season. The images here are not contradictory to each other but create a wondrous kind of oneness and similarity among widely different things, such as the rice field and the ocean.

In the examples we have quoted earlier, notice the use of the em dash and the colon. These are equivalent to the Japanese cutting word 'kireji' and function as a pause and a separation between the two parts of the haiku. When writing in English, which has no such kireji, the em dash and the colon have to be used. Many modern haiku, however, no longer use any of these signs:

> *on the porch*
> *her empty rocker*
> *rocked now by the breeze*
> —Nigel Jenkins[17]

---

17 Nigel Jenkins. *Another Country: Haiku Poetry from Wales* (Gomer Press, 2011), p. 60.

But in their absence, the poets have to carefully construct their haiku so that its two parts, the setting and the body, are clearly differentiated.

In haiku writing, several things must be kept in mind. Gilli says that the haiku poet must avoid using many of the traditional poetic devices such as personification, anthropopathism, anthropomorphism, simile and apostrophe. This is because the haiku follows the principle of 'show, don't tell'. The haiku image shows us a particular incident or what happens at a given moment and never tries to tell us or explain anything about what it shows. It is up to the readers to discover the metaphorical significance and suggestiveness of the image. In *Late-Blooming Cherries*, we have tried to steer clear of any haiku that tries to poeticize and philosophize its subject.

Another very important aspect of the haiku is humour. Because the form is so brief, the humour in it is merely suggested and never explained in so many words. However, as in other poetic forms, the humour in the haiku may also be ironical and thus used as a tool for satire. But whenever a haiku expresses itself in humour, it is no longer called a haiku, but a senryu. The following is a senryu by Kobayashi Issa:

> *all the time I pray to Buddha*
> *I keep on*
> *killing mosquitoes.*[18]

The term 'senryu' was derived from the name of Karai Senryu (1718–90), a haiku poet whose favourite pastime was to collect poems steeped in humour and irony. Therefore, we may say that a senryu also shares the same fundamental elements and chief characteristics of the haiku. It is only the ironic treatment of human nature and the presence of humour that differentiate the two.

Kynpham Sing Nongkynrih

---

18 Kobayashi Issa. *Poems* (PoemHunter.com, 2004), p. 7.

Late-Blooming Cherries

Muskaan Ahuja

Muskaan Ahuja is an IELTS trainer and a teacher of English at Shishu Niketan Public School, Chandigarh. Her haiku have appeared in journals such as *Failed Haiku, Wales Haiku Journal, Bottlerockets, Frogpond, Asahi Haikuist Network, The Haiku Foundation* and *The Cherita*. In 2019, her haiku based on woodblock Japanese prints was displayed at the Bristol Museum and Art Gallery.

crowded bus—
a fly takes
the seat I leave

temple visit
ants on the wall
returning with prasad

gibbous moon
a wild pansy curls up
in the wind

retirement party
a balloon bursts
by itself

forest shadows
... the scurry
of small lives

funeral day—
her off-white saree
so crisp

meeting over—
all the yawns turn
to applause

spinach soup
the child stirs
and stirs the bowl

fallen cherry blossoms
        ... walk
the haiku path

summer evening
a neighbour's kite flying
to the moon

darkening sky
on each mountain
the d   t
              i   t   n
                  s   a   s
                            r

Priti Aisola

Priti is a homemaker who writes and paints occasionally. She is the author of the novel *See Paris for Me* (2009). She has written a spiritual travelogue, *Beyond the Gopurams* (2014); two books of poetry, *A Dinner Invitation to God* (2016) and *O Shrineless Silence* (2017); and a work of creative non-fiction, *Letters to Maya* (2020). Her haiku have appeared in journals such as *Cattails, Failed Haiku, haikuKATHA* and *Under the Bashō*. She lives in Hyderabad.

a wall collapses—
sunflowers
in full view

oil lamp
adrift on a river—
homecoming

sun rays—
the underside of leaves
still dark

silverfish
in a bookcase—
new maps emerge

custard apple—
the squirrel crafts
a bowl

G. Akila

G. Akila is a corporate professional. Her haiku have appeared in journals and anthologies such as *Brass Bell Journal*, *haikuKATHA*, *Haibun Today*, *Sonic Boom*, *Red River Book of Haibun*, *Issa's Untidy Hut*, *Creatrix*, *The Narrow Road Journal*, *Shape of a Poem—An Anthology*. She lives in Hyderabad.

on and off
fireflies
... mood swing

last leaf ...
what does it take
to let go?

bedtime story
she asks me to be louder
for the stars

reunion—
the bamboo grove bursts
with babblers

lip-locked clouds the aftertaste of rain

Sanjuktaa Asopa

Sanjuktaa is primarily a homemaker, though she helps in her family business. In 2016, she co-edited *Naad Anunaad: An Anthology of Contemporary World Haiku*. Her haiku have appeared in journals and anthologies such as *Shiki Kukai*, *Cattails*, *The Heron's Nest*, *Acorn*, *A Hundred Gourds*, *Frogpond*, *The Mainichi*, *Jumble Box*, *World Haiku Review*, *Behind the Mask: Haiku in the Time of Covid-19* and *Failed Haiku*. She lives in Belgaum, Karnataka.

calm waters—
a duck glides over
the morning star

paper boat
big enough to hold
a dream or two

sinking sun ...
the grey of the rocks
deepens again

mulberry silk—
cocooned in the fragrance
of grandma

rocking chair
back and forth between
now and then

the sky trapped
between the mountain peaks—
a hawk's cry

how much rain
you can hold ...
curled autumn leaf

periwinkles—
the joy of being
ordinary

lockdown city
I almost hear
the evening dew

meditation mat
I check for
the invisible ants

all that I want
to tell you tonight ...
glass bangles

opening the window
to a moth and what's left
of the moon

flinging the raindrops
far and wide—
flip-flops

last sparks
from the dying embers ...
my hands in his

R. Suresh Babu

R. Suresh Babu teaches English in Jawahar Navodaya Vidyalaya, Chikkamagaluru. His haiku have appeared in journals such as *Cattails, Failed Haiku, Wales Haiku Journal, Akitsu, Presence, Under the Bashō, Poetry Pea Journal and Podcast, The Asahi Shimbun, World Haiku Series, The Mamba, kontinuum, Haikuniverse, Cold Moon Journal, Chrysanthemum, tsuri-dōrō* and *The Mainichi*. He lives in Chikkamagaluru, Karnataka.

the sky
rolling on a lotus leaf—
dewdrop

spring festival—
the yellow pollen
on her nose ring

granddaughter's birthday—
the candles and cake
virtual

left out
of the wreath—
a dead flower

wedding anniversary—
daughter gifts me
a nodding doll

Ram Chandran

Ram Chandran is a corporate lawyer by profession. His haiku have appeared in journals such as *Modern Haiku, The Heron's Nest, Kingfisher Journal, Cicada's Cry, Failed Haiku, tsuri-dōrō, World Haiku Review, The Mainichi, Haiku Dialogue, The Bamboo Hut, Stardust Haiku* and *kontinuum*. He lives in Madurai, Tamil Nadu.

spring's arrival—
lots of snowflakes
left in my poems

slurping water
from the stream ...
the taste of mountain

plucking rose petals—
the floor full of
strewn thoughts

starry night—
I adore
the twinkles in her eyes

the same moon
when we first met
and now, as we part

misty morning—
sipping
the unfinished dream

thousands of years
in my pocket—
pebbles

night fishing—
the boatman's song
reaching for the moon

Mallika Chari

Mallika Chari is an artist who loves colouring on any surface—fabric, canvas, stones and tree bark. Her haiku have appeared in journals such as *Wildplum*, *Wales Haiku Journal*, *Presence*, *Prune Juice*, *Chrysanthemum*, *Cicadas Cry*, *Frogpond* and *Failed Haiku*. Her haiga have appeared in *Daily Haiga* and *Haigaonline*. She lives in Chennai.

loud tides
disturbed mind
becoming silent

lake
crane and I
fishing companion

spring
grandma's hands hold
Jasmine scent

muddy road
along the tyre marks
I follow the black ants

night ritual
I practise the smile of
Mona Lisa

flood
on the uprooted tree
the same birds

cloudy days
behind her closed eyes
a silver lining

paddy field
the wet soil holds
a folk song

night wind
the unbolted door
a rhythmic thump

waterfall
the soft algae cling
to the rocks

foreign land
among unknown sounds
my mother tongue

Geetashree Chatterjee

Geetashree Chatterjee works in a Fortune 500 Company. An active blogger, her poems and haiku have appeared in various journals and e-zines. Her collection of short stories, *A Basketful of Lies*, was published in 2018. She lives in Delhi.

meditation
   silencing
the cuckoo's call

unswayed
by the breeze
crescent moon

sterile corridors
footsteps follow
mother's baby talk

crammed inside
the medicine chest
whispered prayers

mustard field
the wish to be
my own self

Kanchan Chatterjee

Kanchan Chatterjee is a superintendent of taxes, Goods & Services Tax department, Jamshedpur, Jharkhand. He is the author of *Scattered Leaves* (2020), a collection of haiku. His haiku and haibun have appeared in journals such as *Wales Haiku Journal*, *Frogpond*, *Modern Haiku*, *World Haiku Review*, *Presence*, *Chrysanthemum*, *Cattails*, *The Heron's Nest*, *Asahi Haikuist Network*, *The Mainichi* and others.

just as
the sutra chant begins—
a cuckoo's call

cold day—
from the next room
clipping nails

end of a festival
the dog sniffs
an empty bin

Diwali—
among the wine bottles
a laughing Buddha

between thunderbolts—
the front door's
soft creak

evening chill—
a paper plane stuck
on a barbed wire

long day—
the lonely seagull's
deep arc

morning mist—
beyond it, the cry
of a quail

shimmering heat—
the fish hawker
silent under a shade

village fair—
the tea seller sells
parakeets too

autumn rains—
in the field, a half-sunk
paper boat

Salil Chaturvedi

Salil Chaturvedi is a poet and fiction writer. His haiku have appeared in journals such as *Modern Haiku*, *Frogpond*, *The Heron's Nest*, *Acorn*, *Hedgerow* and *Chrysanthemum*. His haiga have been featured in *Haiku Masters*, a television programme on NHK, Japan. Salil won the Jane Reichhold Memorial Haiga Contest, 2020. His most recent work is *Love and Longing in the Anthropocene—Poems and Haibun* (2022). He lives in Chorao, Goa.

ill in bed
the smell of summer grass
in the dog's paw

bodhi tree
not a single leaf
is still ...

roof repair
my bed partner
the half-moon

summer moon—
the bald heads of
old friends

thunder
inside a curled leaf
the cocoon shifts

border sunset—
soldiers watch
the migrating birds

final goodbye
the ice melts
in her lemonade

squirrel's hop—
the distance travelled
since my childhood

Anannya Dasgupta

Anannya Dasgupta is a poet and photographer. She directs the Centre for Writing and Pedagogy at Krea University, Andhra Pradesh. Her haiku, haiga and haibun have appeared in journals such as *Sonic Boom*, *Failed Haiku*, *World Haiku Review*, *Wales Haiku Journal*, *Prune Juice*, *Right Hand Pointing*, *Drifting Sands Haibun*, *Contemporary Haibun Online* and *Cattails*. She lives in Chennai.

making a plaything
of mountains and rivers—
aerial maps

out of place—
shallow graves
on a riverbank

this journey
to make alone—
the rising sun

prayer—
our fingers
intertwined

on a weighing scale—
the lightness of joy
the heaviness of sorrow

Shashi Angelee Deodhar

Shashi Angelee Deodhar (1947–2018) was an ophthalmologist-turned-haiku poet and haiga artist from Chandigarh. She was a member of the Haiku International Association, Japan; the Haiku Society of America; Haiku Canada; and several other societies. Her works and edited works include *Indian Haiku: A Bilingual Anthology of Haiku by 105 Poets from India* (2008) and *Journeys: An Anthology of International Haibun* (2015) in three volumes. She also translated six books of haiku from English to Hindi.

in the silence
of the zendo
my stomach growls

between us
vapours from the teacups
autumn chill

midnight walk
the dog nudges me down
our moonlit path

out of the fog
a crow's cracked caw
drips into silence

winter-bare tree
ice crystals sculpt
an abandoned nest

gibbous moon
my ear on the curve
of her belly

last night's rain
the birdbath full
of sparrows

a light breeze
the moon in the birdbath
shivers

sudden blackout
so many fireflies
in the garden

pail in hand
I trace the muddy path
of childhood mushrooms

in the monastery
rising above the plainchant
a warbler's half note

Kanjini Devi

Kanjini Devi has been a yoga teacher since 1992. Her haiku have appeared in journals and anthologies such as *The Helping Hand Haiku Anthology*, *NZPS Anthology 2020*, *Prune Juice*, *The Haiku Foundation* and *Oriental Poetry 2020*. She lives in the Far North of Aoteraoa, New Zealand.

framed between
frangipani and a hedge
the photographer

queuing
around the block
weekly supplies and smiles

shooting season
a pair of mallards shuffle
to the old pond

sharing
a private joke
the donkey's grin

loved ones
hovering by the door
touch-and-go

Baisali Chatterjee Dutt

Baisali Chatterjee Dutt is a drama teacher at Sri Sri Academy, Kolkata. Her haiku have appeared in anthologies and journals such as *Cold Moon Journal*, *Haikuniverse*, *Haiku Dialogues*, *The Haiku Foundation*, *Poetry Pea*, *Summer Journal*, *Failed Haiku*, *Haiku in Action* and *haikuKATHA*. Her latest verse novella is *Three Is a Lonely Number*.

skywards
in prayer
... sunflowers

the whirling dervish
blurs into light
... white lotus

skyscrapers—
tombstones erected
on Gaia's bones

ma's wedding bangle
now on my wrist ...
circle of love

candlelight
in his eyes
a flicker of desire

Kinshuk Gupta

Kinshuk Gupta is a medical student at Maulana Azad Medical College, New Delhi. He edits poetry for *Jaggery Lit* and *Mithila Review* and is an associate editor with *Usawa Literary Review*. His poetry and haiku have appeared in journals and newspapers such as *The Hindu, The Times of India, The Quint, Live Mint, Outlook* magazine, *Modern Haiku, Haiku Foundation, Human/Kind Journal, Akitsu Quarterly, World Haiku Review, The Cicada's Cry, Wales Haiku Journal, The Haiku Foundation* and *Contemporary Haibun Online*. He was awarded the inaugural Dr Anamika Poetry Prize (2022) and shortlisted for the Srinivas Rayparol Poetry Prize (2021). He lives in New Delhi.

postal stamps ...
the zigzag edges
of our marriage

loneliness—
my mother fills her room
with incense smoke

autumn evening ...
carving the shadows
into birds

dissection hall—
can I steal a kidney
for my mother?

summer memories—
a fish shoal
ripples the river

cancer ward—
at last the moon
decides to leave

shifting home—
for a moment, the whiff
of dad's sweat

mastectomy—
she orders lamb breasts
for breakfast

Lakshmi Iyer

Lakshmi Iyer is a homemaker. Her haiku have appeared in anthologies and journals such as *haikuKATHA*, *Under the Bashō*, *Brass Bell*, *Whiptail*, *Poetry Pea*, *Failed Haiku*, *The Haiku Foundation*, *Bloo Outlier* and *Cattails*. She is the co-editor of *amber i pause*, a Dhanyavaad Anthology of Triveni Haikai India. She lives in Kerala.

kite flying
I set free
my inhibitions

autumn breeze
another tiny cradle tied
to the temple tree

train journey
the gibbous moon
slips on my pillow

concrete jungle
banyan tree droop
with cement

first colouring book
sun rises with an orange
straw cap

Rohini Gupta

Rohini Gupta is a writer of haiku, fiction and non-fiction. She published *Where Rivers Meet*, a haikai collection, in 2022. She also edited *Fuga No Makoto*, an anthology celebrating ten years of the *World Haiku Review*. She is the editor of two haiku magazines, *World Haiku Review* and *Cafe Haiku*. Her haiku have appeared in journals and anthologies such as *The Heron's Nest*, *The Mainichi*, *Breathing the Same Air Anthology*, *Pins on a Map Anthology*, *Bottlerockets*, *Thunder of the River Renku*, *Journal of Renga and Renku*, *Muse India*, *Stardust*, *Cattails*, *Chrysanthemum*, *Whiskers and Purrs*, *Bloo Outlier Journal* and *Between Sips of Cutting Chai Anthology*. She lives in Mumbai.

single cricket
labouring to fill
the whole city

peering
from the tangle of jasmine
kitten eyes

summer road
the freedom of not knowing
where you are going

both reflected
the white lake palace
and the dark one

Himalayan sun
the lizard and I
share a rock

across the page
faster than my pen
a falcon's shadow

poem interrupted
the wind blows me
a flower

every day
more spring flowers
and virus deaths

butterfly
if only I could replace
the flower I plucked

sleeping
on the marigold offerings
the temple cat

last year's
group photograph
only I remain

foreign country
trying to translate
what's on the plate

waiting for dinner
the kittens curl up
in the bowls

vacation's end
my small black notebook
brings home the mountains

summer reading
the wind flutters
to the last page

temple ruins
only the wind still
offers flowers

light rain
the red rose
overflows

dawn comes
too soon
I lose the stars

cloud shadows—
drifting across the valley
field by field

dawn over Dal Lake
emerging from the mist
the flower boat

Surashree Joshi

Surashree Joshi works as a freelance English trainer, translator and content developer. She is also a trained Hindustani classical vocalist. Her haiku have appeared in journals such as *Failed Haiku, The Haiku Dialogue, Cold Moon Journal, Sonic Boom* and *Prune Juice*. She lives in Pune, Maharashtra.

sickle moon—
somewhere a farmer
kills himself

howling winds—
all I hear
is your heartbeat

her eyes—
I find my resolve
weakening

autumn dusk ...
I cling to the warmth
of your fingers

autumn twilight—
my father asks me
about my father

Abhay K.

Abhay K. is an Indian poet-diplomat. He is the author of ten poetry books, including *The Alphabets of Latin America* (2020), *The Magic of Madagascar* (2021) *and Monsoon* (2022), and the editor of *CAPITALS* (2017), *The Bloomsbury Anthology of Great Indian Poems* (2019), *New Brazilian Poems* (2019), *The Bloomsbury Book of Great Indian Love Poems* (2020) and *The Book of Bihari Literature* (2022). His poems have appeared in over a hundred literary magazines, including *Poetry Salzburg Review* and *Asia Literary Review*. His poem 'Earth Anthem' has been translated into over 150 languages. He received the SAARC Literary Award 2013 and was invited to record his poems at the Library of Congress, Washington, DC, in 2018. His translations of

Kalidasa's *Meghaduta* (2021) and *Ritusamhara* (2021) from Sanskrit have won the KLF Poetry Book of the Year Award 2020–21. He currently serves as India's Ambassador to Madagascar.

a boa clings tightly
to a tree twig—
forest fire

five egrets
flying home—
darkening sky

admiring
its own reflection—
a heron at Mare Masai

stretching its arms
in prayer—
a traveller's palm

world
keep all your wealth
happy watching hoopoes

happy
then sad watching
silky sifakas

hey, butterfly
hide somewhere
storm

purple jacaranda
blooming everywhere
where are you?

breaking
the night's silence
—Scops owls

dawn or dusk
always hooting—
long-tailed ground roller

bare tree twigs
piercing the blue sky
—winter in Tana

Sushama Kapur

Sushama Kapur is an ESL/ EFL trainer and teacher by profession. Her haiku have appeared in journals such as *The Haiku Foundation, Asahi Haikuist Network, Failed Haiku, Cold Moon Journal, Cattails, Ribbons* and *Wales Haiku Journal*. She lives in Pune, Maharashtra.

autumn dusk
the park fills up
with silence

apple crunch
the summer sun
in every bite

eerie silence
tapping my window
a dry branch

long vigil
both the birds and I
await dawn

mountain trek—
under the circling shadow
of a lammergeier

Arvinder Kaur

Arvinder Kaur worked as an associate professor in English literature and media studies and retired as the principal of Government College, Derabassi, Punjab. Her published work includes translations of prose and poetry. She has four collections of haiku poetry to her credit. Her haiku have appeared in journals such as *Frogpond, The Heron's Nest, Modern Haiku, The Mainichi, Asahi Shimbun Network, Femku Mag, Failed Haiku* and *Cold Moon Journal*. She lives in Chandigarh.

unable to bear
the weight of rain
cherry petals

the jacaranda
bereft of petals
quarantine ends

deadlines
for now, the lullaby
of gentle waves

father's spectacles
on a dusty side table
unsolved crossword

how random
the shape of things to come
dandelions

mother's funeral
the breeze gently
caresses my hair

beach sands
the waves take my name
back to the ocean

all the ways
you hide your pain
rounds of coffee

the gentle swing
of a poppy
hopping bees

a summer
that never was …
holidays

courtroom
how white the shirt
of the rapist

self-isolation
moon in the attic window
watching over me

house sale
the last trip
to mama's kitchen

psychiatry clinic
the entire staff
in blue

funeral day
grandpa's chessmen
back in the box

sex education
grandma begins
from the forbidden apple

rain timpani
the pianist's fingers
silent on the ivories

return trip
mother's ashes
in the boat's wake

kite flying
still learning the skill
to let go

rice fields
the coolness of a mud path
to the shrine

Suhit Kelkar

Suhit Kelkar is a journalist whose factual and imaginative writings have appeared in publications in India and abroad. He has two chapbooks of poems and haiku. His haiku and senryu have appeared in journals such as *The Heron's Nest, The Punch Magazine* and *A Hundred Gourds*. He lives in Mumbai.

a mango leaf
the entire world
of the unnamed bug

crossroads
I wait for the cool wind
to go first

the dog's leash
in its own mouth
I recall my obsessions

missing having
a pet at my heels
noonday shadow

seller of sweets
a trunk full
of memories

Ravi Kiran

Ravi Kiran is an electronic engineer and a working professional. His haiku have appeared in journals such as *The Heron's Nest, Modern Haiku, Frogpond, Failed Haiku, Poetry Pea, Presence, tsuri-dōrō, Cattails* and *Prune Juice*. He lives in Hyderabad.

finding its way
through the bylanes
a migrant's song

setting sun
colours fade
silhouettes remain

trail's end
the wind continues
between the pines

long after
the miscarriage
stretch marks

almost dawn
still searching for
the right words

Anju Kishore

Anju Kishore was formerly a professional accountant. She is the author of '*...and I Stop to Listen*', a collection of poetry. She has edited more than half-a-dozen poetry anthologies over the last three years. She is a member of Triveni Haikai, India, and her haiku and haibun have appeared in *haikuKATHA* and *The Heron's Nest*. She lives in Chennai.

crescent moon
the sharp edge
of longing

homeless boy
the lake wears
a tattered sky

pressed rose
the paths
that did not cross

half a rainbow
our marriage
loses its way

bombed homes—
talks go round and round
the table

Neha R. Krishna

Neha R. Krishna is a writer and social media consultant. She is the author of *No Urgency to Be Home* (2022), a collection of haiku and tanka poetry. Her haiku have appeared in journals such as *Under the Bashō, Presence, Frogpond, Failed Haiku, Human/Kind Journal, Frameless Sky, Haiku Foundation, Bones Journal, Prune Juice, Moonbathing Journal, Wild Plum Journal, Asahi Haiku Network* and *Contemporary Haibun Online*. She won the Weighing Raindrops Haiku Contest organized by *Narrow Road* and Glass House Festival 2020. She lives in Mumbai.

night raga
 the moon
  entangled in a tree

subway station
I wish to go
nowhere

rear-view mirror
a hurried look
at the past

a ripple
in the pond
moon shivers

litchi candy
another season
on my tongue

sparrow's first flight
every hour
dad's call

sea breeze
 the scent of your skin
on my tongue

first date
loose thread on his sweater
takes all my attention

Shobhana Kumar

Shobhana Kumar runs an NGO that works with vulnerable communities, especially women and transgenders. She is an associate editor at Yavanika Press and co-curator of *The Quarantine Train*. She has authored seven books ranging from biographies to industrial and corporate histories. She has two collections of poems and a book of haibun titled *A Sky Full of Bucket Lists* (2021), shortlisted for the Touchstone Distinguished Book Awards and awarded the Rabindranath Tagore Literary Prize, 2021–22. She lives in Coimbatore, Tamil Nadu.

meditation
learning to focus
despite pins and needles

terrace garden
the money plant
trails into the neighbour's

lost in thought
an autumn leaf dances
to its fall

abandoned shrine
the gods as lost
as us

size nine
so many miles
in the same shoes

darkened path
the tree erupts
with fireflies

snakes and ladders
in tune with my
career graph

monsoon shower
the night you taught me
how to kiss

year-end
at the wishing fountain
again ...

harvest song
a cradle rocks
under a mango tree

airport trolleys
the hidden stories
of suitcases

Johannes Manjrekar

Johannes Manjrekar (1957–2020) was a scientist, teacher, photographer and poet. His haiku have appeared in journals such as *World Haiku Review, Frogpond, Whirligig, TempsLibres, Cattails* and *The Little Magazine*. He was an active member of the haiku community in India and facilitated several workshops on writing haiku with school and college students over the years. He co-edited the *First Katha Book of Haiku, Senryu, Tanka and Haibun* (2020).

magpie robin—
five minutes of song
fill the whole day

October night—
no answer, but the cricket
doesn't stop

tattered clouds—
the moon's whiteness is
icier tonight

cool breeze—
a thousand things undone
I watch the moon

early moon ...
but now
the traffic

my bare porch—
I silently join
in the neighbours' laughter

passing bus—
the dragonfly readjusts
its balance

red poppies ...
the butterfly always just
out of reach

midnight—
only jasmine now
and cricket song

procession—
the gods march
behind a flag

stalled traffic
a cow picks flowers
off the wedding car

morning mist
the iora is gone
before I recall its name

a moment ago
the moon was balanced
on a telephone wire

curfew—
advertising signs
for nobody

dawn haze—
the bulbul's trills
so clear

veins of lightning
split the sky—
the smell of wet earth

gust of wind
a woman's face lit up
by the cooking fire

Daipayan Nair

Daipayan Nair writes haiku and tanka poems. His collection of haiku, *tilt of the winnowing fan*, was published in 2022. His poems have appeared in journals such as *Haiku Dialogue*, *Haiku in Action*, *haikuKATHA*, *Frogpond* and *Cattails*. He lives in Silchar, Assam.

coloured pebbles
all that's left
in the fishbowl

final bargain—
a cracked egg
in the carton

perfect balance—
the man head-loads a basket
of dried fish

spring morning—
the sweeper stops to pick
a jujube

not letting go
of mum's palm
the coriander leaves

humming an oldie
she removes her bindi
from the mirror

kissing grandma—
the rust on her
brass bangles

childhood
the cigarette
I chew

Priya Narayanan

Priya Narayanan is an interior architect. Her poems and haiku have appeared in journals such as *The Indian Quarterly, Narrow Road Literary Journal, The Bombay Literary Magazine, Modern Haiku, tinywords, Cattails* and *Akitsu Quarterly*. She lives in Ahmedabad.

pillow talk
there's nothing I miss more
now that you're gone

potter's clay
is it
what it is?

beach vacation
the child digs
her own ocean

powdered pangolin scales
the smell
of a dead warrior

empty sky—
how heavy this jar
filled with your ashes

Indra Neil

Indra Neil is a radiologist. His haiku have appeared in journals such as *The Heron's Nest, Presence, Frogpond, Modern Haiku, Wales Haiku Journal* and *Cattails*. He lives in Rajamahendravaram, Andhra Pradesh.

autumn wind
still fresh, the mark
on his ring finger

the flutter of tents
in place of a lullaby ...
refugee camp

picnic basket
the black ants touching
each other's heads

florist's window
the frantic cursives
of a honeybee

spring rain—
my handprints dissolve
around the sapling

Veterans Day
his hands holding
a 'HOMELESS' placard

Women's Day
after the wishes
she resumes her chores

Valentine's Day—
a young man tightens
his guitar strings

Subir Ningthouja

Subir Ningthouja is a physician. His haiku have appeared in journals such as *The Heron's Nest, ESUJ-Haiku, The Mainichi, The Asahi Shimbun, Serow, Presence, Wales Haiku Journal, Haiku Dialogue, World Haiku Review, haikuKATHA, Failed Haiku, Cold Moon Journal, Contemporary Haibun Online, Drifting Sands Haibun, Bloo Outlier, Time Haiku, MahMight Haiku Journal* and *Haikuniverse*. He lives in Imphal.

blue hills
the wind seeds
a forest

train window
the landscape runs
away from me

evening
a flute's tune swirls
with the mist

lockdown
my hair adopts
hippie fashion

waterfall—
a mountain sings
for the sea

Rimi Nath

Rimi Nath teaches literature at North-Eastern Hill University, Shillong. She is the author of *Kushiara and Other Poems* (2021). Her poems and scholarly articles have appeared in several national and international publications. Her haiku have appeared in journals such as *Wales Haiku Journal, Frogpond, Modern Haiku, World Haiku Review, Asahi Haikuist, Under the Bashō* and *Haiku Canada Review*. She lives in Shillong and Guwahati.

crowd at a graveyard—
the world is
a burial ground

fish in a glass jug:
I dream
of escape

solitude—
a peony
blooms alone

birds in pair—
only people are capable
of separating

flooded river:
the entire village
rushes past

washing my face:
last night's dream
erased

two flowers—
a hand
takes away one

steam from a kettle:
the soul
leaving the body

success—
a lone tree
standing

locked in:
no desire
to be found

forest:
boundless
freedom

candlelights—
dance
of the shadows

red rose:
unnoticed
in a corner

loneliness—
an island
of hapless settlers

masked faces
talking
eyes

balloon in the sky—
severed
from my past

chilly February—
the warmth
of Sohra oranges

cacophony of crows—
discord over
a piece of bread

bird in an open cage—
free
to come back

scribbling at my desk—
a cooing dove
my only companion

Kynpham Sing Nongkynrih

Kynpham Sing Nongkynrih teaches literature at North-Eastern Hill University, Shillong. He is the author of *Around the Hearth: Khasi Legends* (2007), *The Yearning of Seeds* (2011), *Time's Barter: Haiku and Senryu* (2015), *Funeral Nights* (2021) and the co-editor of *Dancing Earth: An Anthology of Poetry from Northeast India* (2009). His haiku have appeared in journals such as *Wales Haiku Journal, Frogpond, Modern Haiku, Simply Haiku, World Haiku Review, Cattails, Presence, The Heron's Nest, Asahi Haikuist Network, Planet: The Welsh Internationalist, Muse India, Kavya Bharati, The Yearning of Seeds, Dancing Earth: An Anthology of Poetry from North-East India* and *The HarperCollins Book of English Poetry*. His awards include the first North-East Poetry Award (Tripura, 2004),

the first Veer Shankar Shah-Raghunath Shah National Award for tribal literature (Madhya Pradesh, 2008), The Bangalore Review June Jazz Award (2021), SPARROW Literary Award (2022) and a Tagore Fellowship (IIAS, Shimla, 2018).

late-blooming cherries
by the highway—how else can I
describe my haiku?

sunset—
watching you
watching

first spring rain
the bus shelter
only half-finished

how hopeful to watch
hip-hops with falling pants
doing a traditional dance

rain for days—
only soldiers' clothes flapping
on a sagging line

Stupas of Sanchi—
a monk under a tree, lost
in a mobile phone

summer morning—
the rain drowns out the music
of a country song

last haiku of Bashō
alone
facing a blank page

stormy afternoon:
on the stump of a cherry
a bulbul

city's cluttered drains
even unwanted infants
are thrown in

yearning—
so many days without hills
in the hot metropolis

abandoned spider's web:
insects keep dying
in it

juicy-looking plums
watery taste—shouldn't have
plucked on a rainy day

autumn leaves falling—
time's barter, dreadful
for humans alone

fiery pomegranate
bursting with ripe seeds—earth
bursting with humans

never knew bulbuls
feeding at dawn, noisy as
Khasi funerals

autumn sky spreading
heaps of cotton wool—all set
to make winter rugs

newly discovered
contagion of modern age—
ear-clutching itch

creepy caterpillar,
when did you become
these flying colours?

region's backwardness
explained by a road sign:
'slow men at work'

Pravat Kumar Padhy

Pravat Kumar Padhy is a retired general manager from Oil and Natural Gas Corporation (ONGC). He is an award-winning poet with seven collections of poetry to his credit. His haiku have appeared in journals and anthologies such as *tsuri-dōrō, Poetry Pea, Indian Kukai, Seashores, Stardust Haiku, Frogpond, Wales Haiku Journal, The Heron's Nest, The Mainichi, Mann Library's Daily Haiku, Haikuniverse* and *Gems: An Anthology of Haiku, Senryu and Sedoka*. He lives in Bhubaneswar.

red carpet—
the monks walk
barefoot

flowing river—
the bereaved girl holds
a palmful of water

sunrise—
the morning enters
without knocking

thick clouds—
a gap takes me
to the ocean

street dog—
an old man shares
his silence

braided hair—
the breeze shaping
the waterfall

motherhood—
how tenderly clouds
hold the rain

frozen pond—
the missing sound
of skipping stones

Aparna Pathak

Aparna Pathak is a freelance editor associated with a web newspaper. Her haiku have appeared in journals such as *Frogpond, Golden Triangle Haiku, Presence, Acorn, tinywords, Mayfly, Cattails, The Heron's Nest, Modern Haiku* and *Blithe Spirit*. She won first prizes at the Sonic Boom Senryu Contest (2018) and The Haiku Association's Three Rivers Fourth Haiku Contest (2018). She lives in Gurugram, Haryana.

pumpkin soup
the family's oneness
in slurps

late autumn—
the weight of being
unburdened

autumn river
if only I had tied
the boat

hopscotch
square to square
the refugee girl

after all the promises
not to overdo the role
—walrus moustache

Vandana Parashar

Vandana Parashar is an associate editor of *haikuKATHA* and *Poetry Pea*. She has published two haiku chapbooks, *I Am* and *Alone, I Am Not*. Her haiku have appeared in journals such as *Haiku Dialogue, haikuKATHA, tsuri-dōrō, The Haiku Foundation* and *Human/Kind Journal*. She lives in Panchkula, Haryana.

ebbing tide
more and more
of me revealed

bare tree
who will miss me
when I am gone?

hunger strike
by the end of the day
hunger strikes

receding flood
a still cow still
tethered

wildflower
they say I am not
ambitious

peace memorial
I walk a mile
in father's shoes

how many more
clouds will pass before it rains
—miscarriage

unexpected showers
every puddle sets free
the child in me

Shalini Pattabiraman

Shalini Pattabiraman teaches English at a secondary school. She is an associate editor of *Triveni Haikai Journal* and co-moderates *The Haibun Gallery*. Her haiku have appeared in journals such as *Haiku Dialogue, Akita Haiku, Wales Haiku Journal* and *The Blōō Outlier Journal*. She won the Ken and Noragh Jones Award for haibun writing in 2020, organized by the British Haiku Society. She lives in Dundee, Scotland.

busy hands—
a loom lulls
the baby to sleep

dark woods
only light can burrow
with the rabbits

evening news
only the birds
arrive home

fading urn ...
even squiggles
were words once

under caterpillar feet, a trembling leaf

Madhuri Pillai

Madhuri Pillai is a retired journalist who now spends more and more time on her animal causes. Her haiku have appeared in journals such as *tinywords*, *Asahi Haikuist Network*, *The Heron's Nest*, *Frogpond*, *Modern Haiku*, *Chrysanthemum*, *Cattails*, *Presence*, *Failed Haiku*, *A Hundred Gourds*, *Bottle Rocket*, *Wild Plum Journal*, *Akitsu Quarterly*, *Under the Bashō* and *Muse India*. She lives in Melbourne, Australia.

temple bells ...
after the crescendo
the cicadas

frost on the grass
the slippery slope
of old friendships

fading summer
still humming the hymn
night mosquitoes

siblings ...
the different narratives
of our childhood

moonless ...
a cat's snarl
startles the night

remembering her ...
the cyclamen
gets another feed

berceuse ...
all afternoon
the mourning dove

lost dog
I leave my voice
in every street

Amrutha Prabhu

Amrutha Prabhu is a computer engineer. Her haiku have appeared in journals such as *Ribbons, The Haiku Foundation, Cold Moon Journal, Kontinuum, Haikuniverse, The Mamba, Nick Virgilio Haiku, Failed Haiku, Contemporary Haibun Online, Presence, tsuri-dōrō, Poetry Pea, Bull Headed, Triya, Trash Panda, Asahi Haikuist Network, Freshout Magazine, MahMight Haiku Journal, Drifting Sands, Cafe Haiku, South Wales Evening News* and *Haiku Canada*. She lives in Bengaluru.

I bite
the crescent moon ...
summer melon

neatly arranged next to
a temple doormat ...
dirty shoes

long silence—
his unsaid words
filled my heart

still winter night—
the clock and I
still working

slow stream—
an ant on
a leaf boat

Raamesh Gowri Raghavan

Raamesh Gowri Raghavan teaches epigraphy at INSTUCEN Trust and the Asiatic Society of Mumbai, and conducts peer counselling for suicide prevention for organizations like Pawsitive Synergies. His haiku have appeared in journals such as *GloMag, Whispers, Ardea, Ershik, Miriam's Well, A Hundred Gourds, Shamrock, Cattails, Chrysanthemum, World Haiku Review* and *Issa's Untidy Hut*. He lives in Thane, Maharashtra.

summer lull
waiting for jamuns
to ripen

frog pond
—a new croak
joins the chorus

mother's song
the pressure cooker
hums with her

saltless soup
I grow a day older
without you

yellow leaves
grandma sweeps up
yesterday's storm

Brijesh Raj

Brijesh Raj is a veterinary acupuncturist and one of the editors at *Cafe Haiku*. He and his wife run the Tai-Qi Touch, an internationally recognized Tai Chi Qigong training institute. His haiku have appeared in journals and anthologies such as *World Haiku Review, Narrow Road, Cattails, The Heron's Nest, Failed Haiku* and *Naad Anunaad*. He lives in Mumbai.

winter in the hills
even the sun
sleeps in late

fissured fields
watering the crop
with his tears

chewing gum—
the way you stretch
an ar-gu-men-t

no moon
that night our eyes
wouldn't meet

family reunion
the widest smile
the counsellor's

chainsaw
the strident wail
of falling trees

forest walk
the cool breath
of Eucalyptus trees

cold morning
each cat finds
its own patch of sun

Geethanjali Rajan

Geethanjali Rajan is the haiku editor at *Cattails* and teaches English and Japanese at various organizations as a language consultant. She is the author of a book of haiku, *Unexpected Gift* (2021). Her e-book of collaborative rengay with Sonam Chhoki (Bhutan) was shortlisted for The Touchstone Distinguished Book Award. *Fragments of Conversation*, another e-book of collaborative rengay, is forthcoming. Her haiku have appeared in journals such as *Chrysanthemum, World Haiku Review, A Hundred Gourds, The Mainichi, tinywords, Under the Bashō, Muse India, Asahi Haikuist Network, Sonic Boom, Blithe Spirit, Wales Haiku Journal, Brass Bell: A Haiku Journal* and *Yamadera Bashō*. In 2013, she won the Raedleaf Poetry India Award. She lives in Chennai.

Pongal
her anklets follow
a cowbell's tinkle

a lone tree
shares a barren field—
childhood home

hospital stay—
outside my window
another leaf falls

last night's storm—
mother sweeps away
the broken nest

clear sky—
the vendor sells clouds
of cotton candy

childhood song—
the rhythm of women
threshing grain

blue gum
I taste a mouthful
of mountain air

hidden moon
the nimble hands
of a mehendi artist

cloudburst
another node shows up
in the scan

hearing aid—
grandma now complains
about the squirrels

everyday yoga
the single-leg balance
of here and there

a handful of rice
at the end of the day—
harvest moon

silent mountain path—
the continued chatter
in my mind

harvest moon ...
two fallow farms
lie side by side

New Year wish
the wingspan
of a white egret

morning tea—
sharing the veranda
with a ring-necked parrot

afternoon heat
after the rumble of a bus
more heat

almost dusk
only paper flowers
in the autumn wind

noon stillness—
the clatter of coins
in the beggar's bowl

milkweed fluff
setting afloat
a daydream

Milan Rajkumar

Milan Rajkumar teaches economics at a secondary school. His haiku have appeared in journals such as *Modern Haiku, Seabeck Haiku Anthology, The Cicadas Cry, Under The Bashō, Cattails, Prune Juice, The Heron's Nest, Contemporary Haibun Online, Wales Haiku Journal, Presence, Frameless Sky, Creatrix, Autumn Moon Haiku Journal, Asahi Haikuist Network, The Mainichi, Cold Moon Journal, The Mumba Journal, The Quills, Akitsu Quarterly, Frogpond, Ribbons, tsuri-dōrō, Chrysanthemum, Earth Rise, Kyoto Haiku Project, Stardust Haiku, Brass Bell, Bamboo Hut, White Enso, Otoroshi, Poetry Pea, Failed Haiku* and *Haiku Foundation*. He lives in Imphal.

weaving
for the next life—
a caterpillar

hot noon
the sweet seller and flies
nap together

far from home—
a bowl of bamboo shoots
in a cookbook

dry fields ...
rice planting songs
lost in the wind

school reopening—
on cobwebbed blackboard
last year's lesson

mother's day—
for mama's old photo
a new frame

waves
of butterflies in the sky—
plum blossoms!

autumn evening
on the courtesan's earrings
the moon's reflection

K. Ramesh

K. Ramesh teaches at the J. Krishnamurti School in Chengalpattu, near Chennai. He writes haiku, tanka and free verse. His works have appeared in journals and anthologies such as *Modern Haiku, Presence, Frogpond, The Heron's Nest, The Mainichi, Acorn, tinywords, The Mamba Journal* and *NHK Haiku Masters*. He has written three haiku collections: *Soap Bubbles* (2007), *From Pebble to Pebble* (2014) and *A Small Tree of Tender Leaves* (2020). He lives in Chengalpattu.

power failure—
closing the book
I listen to the rain

summer afternoon
a pail with rope rests
on the rim of a well

a yellow leaf
touching the green ones
on its way down

cloudy afternoon—
a chrysanthemum blooms
in the paper folder's hand

railway station ...
a banyan tree's roots
yet to reach the ground

morning rain ...
the long gap between
two sips of tea

camera in my hands ...
the shoulder bag
so light

shadow of a fish ...
from pebble
to pebble

a twitter brings me
to the window ...
full moon

summer morning ...
a garden lizard drinks
the dewdrop on a leaf

summer afternoon ...
no break
for the coppersmith

winter night ...
mother and I search
for a pill on the floor

daybreak ...
I drink tea facing
the hill's silence

abandoned dog
looking at the face of
every pedestrian

full moon—
everything in its place
in the kitchen

dawn ...
amid bird calls
sound of a broom

dawn
I come face to face
with a mountain

no breeze ...
children on branches
sway their legs

scent of blossoms ...
her house at the end
of the avenue

conversation over
I touch a petal ...
real blossoms

Kala Ramesh

Kala Ramesh, the founder and director of TRIVENI Haikai India, is an editor, anthologist and external faculty member of Symbiosis International University, Pune, where she has been teaching a haikai course since 2012. She is the author of *Haiku & A Companion Activity Book* (2010), *Beyond the Horizon Beyond* (2017) and *The Forest I Know* (2021). In 2016, she edited *Naad Anunaad: An Anthology of Contemporary World Haiku* as the chief editor. Her haiku have appeared in journals such as *Acorn, Sonic Boom, The Heron's Nest, Wales Haiku Journal, Failed Haiku* and *Bones Journal*. She won the first prize at the Eighth Akita International Haiku Contest and was awarded the WE Trailblazer Poet Award 2020 from Women Empowered—India. She lives in Pune and Chennai.

scented twilight ...
the reason dragonflies
pause in flight

did Ganga dream of being the city's sewage?

coming full circle I stumble over a broken promise

mountain trek
my steps ringed
with birdsong

untidy busker
his guitar
       in perfect pitch

ginko walk
the pause and pauses
of a dragonfly

tinkling bells
cows bring home
the twilight hour

plucked jasmine
a funeral
      on my hands

an eagle shadows a wheat field's yellow whisper

autumn evening
the neighbour's laughter
deepens our silence

who am I
       a falling leaf
gives the answer

spring rain
halfway through my meal
a scoop of loneliness

dawn at low tide ...
have waves left their raga
as shoreline patterns?

dense fog
the train evaporates
into a distant horn

temple redone
       Kali's tongue
not so red

deep in raga ...
        sudden applause
startles the singer

windstorm
a battered scarecrow turns
to a new direction

Gita chanting
        birds become
the ellipsis

lotus leaf ...
a water droplet rolls
the moon

thunderclap—
the darkening sky splits
into liquid night

the year passes
stones on the pathway
only get deeper

paper moon ...
a cliff-diver folds
in the setting sun

morning prayers
the rising sun between
my hands

Srinivas S.

Srinivas S. teaches English at the Rishi Valley School, Andhra Pradesh. His haiku have appeared in journals such as *haikuKATHA, Akita Haiku, Frogpond, Modern Haiku, The Heron's Nest, Presence* and *World Haiku Review*. In 2021, he won prizes at the Vancouver Cherry Blossom Festival and the Akita Haiku Contest. He lives near Madanapalle, Andhra Pradesh.

riverbank
between our silences
a gurgle

neem tree
the conference
of crows

toll booth
no crossing fee
for flower petals

street cricket ...
the window we broke
still broken

train journey ...
the tunnel lengthens
into night

softer
through the sakura
full moon

between waves the life of a footprint

suicide point—
the valley lies in
the fog below

Srinivas Rao Sambangi

Srinivasa Rao Sambangi works for a pharma company. His debut collection of haiku and senryu, *forget-me-nots*, was published in 2022. His haiku have appeared in journals and anthologies such as *Frogpond*, *Modern Haiku*, *Heron's Nest*, *Blithe Spirit*, *Akitsu Quarterly*, *Wales Haiku Journal*, *Autumn Moon*, *Presence*, *Prune Juice*, *Failed Haiku* and *Red Moon Anthology*. In 2022, he won the VCBF haiku contest. He lives in Hyderabad.

walking stick
 I'm a step closer
to the centipede

independence day—
the flower girl carries home
an empty basket

second-hand book
she picks another colour
 to underline

first snow
two banyan roots hold
 an empty swing

sickle moon
grandpa in the street
without a stick

felling the tree
an axe-man takes a break
to eat the mango

sunny morning
I lift the river
in cupped hands

change in the wind
the rain becomes
a song

Minal Sarosh

Minal Sarosh used to work at a bank but is now a full-time writer. She has published two novels, *Soil for My Roots* (2015) and *Wicked Money* (2020), and two poetry collections, *Mitosis and Other Poems* (1992) and *A Lizard's Tail and Other Poems* (2020). Her haiku and senryu have appeared in journals such as *Wales Haiku Journal*, *The Cicada's Cry*, *Poetry Pea Podcast*, *Frameless Sky*, *Frogpond*, *Prune Juice*, *Failed Haiku*, *Haiku Dialogue*, *Haiku Foundation*, *The Bamboo Hut*, *World Haiku Review*, *Cattails*, *tsuri-dōrō* and *Fireflies*. In 2005 she won the Commendation Prize at the All India Poetry Competition, organized by The Poetry Society (India). She has also won prizes at many haiku poetry contests. She lives in Ahmedabad.

moving house
they plant a rose tree where
their dog was buried

lying on the beach
the sun sets between
our toes

cowbells ...
one thought bumping
into another

face mask
the way the ocean
covers the earth

anniversary
she dyes her hair
for the party

chemotherapy
she takes a selfie with
the new wig

insomnia
a map on my
creased pillow

window shopping
she tries to lose weight
for the dress

grandma's tombstone
the black granite stone
reflects my face

banyan tree
I try to get all in the
family picture

passing clouds
what to do
what not to do

Joe Sebastian

Joe Sebastian is a principal commissioner of Income Tax. He has published one collection of haiku, *Myriad Musings*. His haiku have appeared in journals such as *Wales Haiku Journal, Mayfly, Creatrix, Cold Moon Journal, Presence, Haikuniverse, The Haiku Foundation, Asahi Shimbun, Muse India, Haiku Xpressions, The Akitsu Quarterly, Failed Haiku, The Bamboo Hut, Poetry Pea, The Sunflower Collective* and *Stardust Haiku*. He lives in Bengaluru.

deeper than the
hoot of snowy owls
winter solitude

taro leaf
mountain waltzes
in a droplet

newly married—
a new fullness
to the moon

early morning pond
stillness reflected
in stillness

from mirror to mirror
trying to make
the short red dress fit

the day ends as it began
she, on the same side
of the bed

Covid ward
the way
the last leaf clings

late summer
the stream steadily
losing its voice

forest trek
old pines absorb
the city inside me

keeper of
innermost secrets
her Barbie

mirrored
in the baby's eyes
mom's smile

Teji Sethi

Teji Sethi is a nutritionist by profession and freelances in creative writing. She is the founder of *Triya*, a bilingual space for haiku, tanka and micro poems. She has published a collection of haiku and senryu, *Moss Laden Walls* (2021). Her haiku have appeared in journals such as *Under the Bashō, Failed Haiku, The Haiku Foundation, Prune Juice, Cold Moon Journal, Femku Mag, Asahi Shimbun, Poetry Pea, Usawa Literary Review, Cafe Haiku, World Haiku Review, Haikuuniverse, Narrow Road, Ribbons, Drifting Sand, Innsaei, The Heron's Nest, Acorn, Modern Haiku, Wales Haiku Journal, haikuKATHA, Moonbathing Journal, Frameless Sky,*

Cattails, The World Haiku Series, Frogpond and *The Wise Owl Literary Journal*. In 2021, she won the haiku contest organized by Indian Kukai. She has also won prizes at other haiku contests. She lives in Bengaluru.

gunshots
I know nothing
of lullabies

fading sun
an eagle's screech
pierces my melancholy

a turn at fifty
out of nowhere, the battles
I had left behind

temple in ruins
a brook nearby
brims with lotus

crossing borders ...
I carry the weight
of a throbbing silence

season of falling leaves
wherever life
       takes us

ceaseless rains
a patch under the banyan
still dry

as it goes
with the wind, this cherry petal
so shall I

new moon
the stillness of sea
awaits a tide

you and me
together yet apart
beads of a rosary

a tender plant
pushes through the cracks
cemetery

his last trip
on the waters of the Ganges
      a floating urn

autumn breeze ...
her forehead still moist
with the parting kiss

amavasya
my scars eclipsed
for a night

Shloka Shankar

Shloka Shankar is a poet, editor, publisher and self-taught visual artist. Her poems and artwork have appeared in over 200 online and print venues and her haiku have appeared in journals such as *Modern Haiku, Frogpond, Prune Juice, Failed Haiku, Under the Bashō, Acorn, Wales Haiku Journal, tinywords, Hedgerow* and *Whiptail*. In addition, she has edited and co-edited six international poetry anthologies since 2016. She is the founding editor of *Sonic Boom* and its imprint, Yavanika Press. She is the author of *Points of Arrival* (2021), a microchap, and *The Field of Why* (2022), a debut haiku collection. She lives in Bengaluru.

actuarial table
a firefly escapes
from the jar

pewter skies ...
I sink deeper into
a ghazal

autumn deepens ...
I hang another day
on the nail

winter dusk ...
I replace my commas
with full stops

migrating geese, I leave my poem open-ended

a whiff
of what was ...
petrichor

winter evening ...
every thought
a monologue

returning my inner voice to me, creek-song

Kashiana Singh

Kashiana Singh currently serves as a managing editor for *Poets Reading the News*. She has two collections of poetry, *Crushed Anthills* (2020), a chapbook, and a full-length collection, *Woman by the Door* (2022). Her haiku have appeared in journals and anthologies such as *Muse India, Rattle Poetry, Ink Sweat, Narrow Road, Remington Review* and *Tears and Sea Beck Anthology*. She lives in North Carolina, USA.

cradle songs
on the drive home
my empty womb

drifting snowflakes—
I restore the fragile lace
of my wedding veil

another argument
a lavender poultice
under my pillow

shallow breaths—
grandma whispers
a final blessing

one half
of a cockle shell
the receding sea

my mother's
knitted sweaters
I unravel knots

frosty morning
I wear a shawl
of memories

half moon
the cracked surface
of a frozen lake

Neena Singh

Neena Singh is a banker by profession. She runs a non-profit organization in Chandigarh for the education and health of underprivileged children. She has published two collections of poetry, *Whispers of the Soul* (2016) and *One Breath Poetry* (2020). Her haiku and allied poetry have appeared in journals such as *The Heron's Nest, Frogpond, Modern Haiku, Presence, Heliosparrow, The Haiku Foundation, Wales Haiku Journal, Chrysanthemum, The Mamba, Cho, Drifting Sands* and *The Cherita*. She lives in Chandigarh.

quiet mourners
a half-eaten peach
on the table

granny's crooning
awakens the baby
winter sunshine

wooden ladder
on the neighbour's wall
the moon climbs down

autumn dusk
an old friend's hand
in mine

new moon—
mother's story remains
half-told

a moment
becomes a lifetime ...
a firefly in my hand

childhood memories ...
I open and close
the wrought-iron gate

sudden rain ...
I pick magnolia blossoms
from Buddha's lap

summer dusk ...
the old woman gathers
her unsold corn

grasshopper
are you alone too
this autumn eve?

last train home ...
the fishmonger's basket
filled with potatoes

Ram Krishna Singh

Ram Krishna Singh retired as a professor of English from the Department of Humanities and Social Sciences IIT, Indian School of Mines, Dhanbad, Jharkhand. He has published twenty poetry collections, including *Sense and Silence: Collected Poems* (2010), *You Can't Scent Me and Other Selected Poems* (2016), *God Too Awaits Light* (2017), *Growing Within/Desăvârşire lăuntrică* (2017), *There's No Paradise and Other Selected Poems Tanka & Haiku* (2019), *Tainted with Prayers: Contaminado con Oraciones* (2020), *A Lone Sparrow* (2021) and *Against the Waves: Selected Poems* (2021). His haiku have appeared in journals such as *Poetry Pea, Ko, Samobor Haiku*

Meeting, Wales Haiku Journal, The Mainichi, Asahi Haiku Network, Lynx, Ambrosia: Journal of Fine Haiku, World Haiku Review and *Three Line Poetry*. He lives in Dhanbad.

wiping his face—
under the umbrella
an old man with books

old diary—
finding phone numbers
of friends still alive

red with shame
the sky at sunrise
one more kiss

whiff of wine—
remembering the bouquet
she gave me once

tangled together
flames of a double lamp
on the terrace

a lone sparrow
atop the naked branch
viewing sunset

winter holidays—
my son chases butterflies
flower to flower

on the terrace
facing the sun
an empty chair

A. Thiagarajan

A. Thiagarajan retired in 2008 as the deputy chief operating officer of a multinational bank in Mumbai. He writes poems, haiku, short stories and articles in English and Tamil. His haiku have appeared in journals such as *White Lotus, tinywords, Frogpond, Simply Haiku, Moonset Autumn, Modern Haiku* and *The Heron's Nest*. He lives in Mumbai.

no words—
between us
the old duet

evening train ...
an empty lunchbox
on the window seat

hot afternoon
the carter wipes his hand
on the donkey's back

village temple—
kids behind the gods
playing hide-and-seek

new actors—
Gandhi is shot
again

still puddle—
a farm labourer washes her face
with the sky

discarded doll—
my kid wants it back
when taken by another

as the light changes
I rush across pulling
the wrong woman

yoga class
the child looks at mom
upside down

open door—
dawn enters
without ringing

slanted sun
half of her
on half of him

Paresh Tiwari

Paresh Tiwari is a naval officer from Lucknow. He has published three collections of poetry, *An Inch of Sky* (2014), *Raindrops Chasing Raindrops* (2018) and *Now a Poem, Now a Forest* (2022). He co-edited the haibun anthology, *Red River Book of Haibun, Vol. 1* (2019). A Pushcart Prize nominee, his haiku have appeared in journals such as *The Heron's Nest, Frogpond, Modern Haiku, Cattails, Bones Journal, World Haiku Review* and *Daily Haiku*. He lives in Mumbai.

sunset beach—
a parasol leans into
its own shadow

early morning ...
a tree's foliage bursts
into parakeets

fading daylight—
an oarsman's ballad
drifts ashore

mustard fields—
a thimbleful of sun
on each blossom

longest night ...
the taste of sea breeze
and her absence

ceasefire ...
the shuffle of boots and
not much else

in each wrinkle
gran's untold story ...
waning moon

all the ways
to paint a summer sky ...
saxophone blues

prayer flags ...
slowly the snow fills up
my footsteps

cloudless day ...
a field of dried grass
in *italics*

war news ...
the dark underbelly
of autumn clouds

toddler's hideout ...
the azaleas fragrant
with giggles

cloudburst ...
my son adds his voice
to the rumble

the cold tiles
of the waiting room ...
fertility clinic

Anitha Varma

Anitha Varma describes herself as a housewife. She writes poems and haiku. *The Salt of a Distant Sea* (2021) is her first collection of poetry. In 2014, she won a prize at the third Japan–Russia Haiku Contest. Her haiku have appeared in journals and anthologies such as *Cattails, The Heron's Nest, A Hundred Gourds, Presence, Wednesday Haiku, Failed Haiku, tinywords, The Mainichi, Naad Anunaad* and *The Jumblebox*. She lives in Kerala.

missing grandpa
the dusty chessmen
frozen in their moves

a dragonfly
struggles to hold its perch
rainstorm

meandering thoughts
I wander
where my feet take me

hot noon
a column of ants drag
one butterfly wing

ancient temple
the peaceful flutter
of a hundred lamps

day moon
trees overflow
with roosting sounds

deserted ghat
I empty the urn
of your memories

temple festival
the tired eyes of the boy
selling amulets

installation art
I enter a room with
too many windows

insomnia
the night hangs heavy
on my eyelids

the sleeping Buddha
I continue to count sheep
along with the moon

the first wail—
my last resistance
comes crumbling down

dandelion bursts
all those wishes
I scatter in the wind

letting go—
what I learn from the dance
of a maple leaf

Vidya S. Venkatramani

Vidya S. Venkatramani teaches in B-schools and facilitates workshops on behavioural and leadership skills for corporates. Her haiku, haibun and senryu have appeared in journals and anthologies such as *A Hundred Gourds, Cattails, Presence, The Heron's Nest, Wales Haiku Journal, Prune Juice, Under the Bashō, World Haiku Review, Haibun Today, Cafe Haiku, Muse India, Naad Anunaad, Red River Book of Haibun* and *The Wonder Code*. She lives in Chennai.

still noon—
the plop of an overripe mango
on the pavement

migrant worker—
asking the geese
for the way home

meditation
a rock dove inches
closer to me

sacred grove—
trees braided together
with vines and prayers

rain upon rain—
mother's orchids
still facing skywards

sundown—
in the mango tree
the flash of a flameback

muddy puddle—
the stretch of my legs
an inch too short

new home—
the street dog befriends me
sniff by sniff

HarperCollins *Publishers* India

At HarperCollins India, we believe in telling the best stories and finding the widest readership for our books in every format possible. We started publishing in 1992; a great deal has changed since then, but what has remained constant is the passion with which our authors write their books, the love with which readers receive them, and the sheer joy and excitement that we as publishers feel in being a part of the publishing process.

Over the years, we've had the pleasure of publishing some of the finest writing from the subcontinent and around the world, including several award-winning titles and some of the biggest bestsellers in India's publishing history. But nothing has meant more to us than the fact that millions of people have read the books we published, and that somewhere, a book of ours might have made a difference.

As we look to the future, we go back to that one word— a word which has been a driving force for us all these years.

Read.